Acknowledgemen

Firstly, I would like to say a big thank you to the Creator of the Heavens and the Earth for all that He has done for me. He has graced me with the patience and the opportunity to create this book through my experiences of life. This is a gift from myself to humanity. A gift that will help readers shift onto a higher level of consciousness, paving the path to a better quality of life.

Secondly, I want to say a big thank you to all of the people that have supported me with contributions in the making of this book - from the design of the book cover, down to editing of the content and all of the people that have helped me to articulate this concept and philosophy to the world.

Thank you to Paul Van Buren, Darren Casey, Katie Lockwood, Shaz Khan and Keidi Keating. This book wouldn't have been possible without you guys. Thank you to all the names that have not been mentioned, please forgive me but you all know who you are.

I would like to say a huge thank you to YOU. I hope you all gain some insights from this book and that you take away something that'll inspire you to make a positive change in your life...

...and how could I forget the one and only, if it wasn't for this amazing person, I wouldn't even be here today living my best life…my beautiful wife, Melanie Jack. Thank You.

CONTENTS

INTRODUCTION

Welcome to the beginning of an epic journey where you will discover the life-changing power of the force within and learn some all-important universal laws. It isn't a coincidence that you have attracted this book; it's that time in your life where you are shifting in consciousness. This book will be a guide for you to discover the light and power within, create the life you desire and enable you to take a leap into the unknown where all possibilities exist. I am so excited for you! After you've finished reading this book, your life will never be the same. From this moment on there will be a shift in your consciousness. You will start to see life with a different outlook. This, in turn, will shift your vibration to a whole new frequency. Just by reading this vibrational code, you will start to become the powerful being that you were created to be as long as you work on all that is required of you and do not just read without implementing. Knowledge isn't power, but knowledge plus implementation is power.

There are many pieces of life's puzzle in here. Be receptive and open to receive. Be still for the presence of the force of life within. You can't see, taste or touch it, but it's alive and keeps us alive and has our best interests at heart. The force within wants us to evolve and become higher conscious beings, enabling us to use the universal laws and work with both Mother Nature and our Heavenly Father, as above so below.

This book will give a step-by-step guide to true inner freedom, if you put the knowledge and wisdom into action and learn from your experiences along the way. You will gain great wisdom and a deeper understanding of your true self and life, enabling you to start creating the life that you have always dreamed of living.

You are a creator, having been made in the image of The Creator. You have been creating your life unknowingly, rather than knowingly. You've most likely been creating the life you don't want, rather than the one you *do* want, due to lack of knowledge and not knowing the powerful force within and its functions. After all this time, you are going to discover ancient wisdom broken down in simple terms that can—with implementation—transform your life, set you free from the limitations of the world and allow you to live a life with abundance.

This is an inside job—inside out. The journey starts within, no more searching externally in people, material objects, substances, and drama only to feel like life isn't filling the void within. Relying on these things just creates more pain and emptiness. Now is the time to go within, deep within the depths of your soul, to discover who you really are. This enables the world to experience YOU and not the person you've become just to fit in, to be accepted or to feel a belonging. It's so important to be yourself... life works for you when you are being yourself! You have a uniqueness that the world wants to get to know. Many go to the grave without experiencing who they really were because of the pressures of society. Many even commit suicide because they no longer like who they have become and can't stand who they are. I didn't like the person I had become and couldn't stand who I was and what I was doing. I was just a product of my environment and my surroundings as a child where I witnessed violence, crime, drugs and prison. That was my programme and that's all I knew until I suffered so much. The suffering itself had been relentless in helping me discover something that had been with me entire life. It is when I felt I couldn't suffer anymore that I discovered the force within. I had no other option but to die to my old self, surrender to the force and build a relationship with it.

The entire world has been programming and conditioning us from childbirth, feeding us drugs through injections and tagging us with a National Insurance Number. We become conditioned and imprisoned by the world, through our five senses: sight, taste, touch, hearing and smell. We also become conditioned through false beliefs about life and ourselves, who we are, what we are and what we are capable of. These are limiting beliefs the world instils in us, programming us from birth. Our parents have programmed us with all their data and generational soul ties. We have been programmed by the education system, media, by the food we eat, by the culture we come from and religious beliefs, all of which have been designed to keep us as slaves in the programme of conformity.

That's why I am writing this book. It's information for you and your family, to help you shift your life to a whole new level of being. It's no longer me that lives but it's the force that lives in me and I am a vessel of Light to serve humanity, enabling you to say goodbye to the old self and to discover the force within. You are unique and deserve to leave a stamp on Earth, before your departure, as life is so short and precious, and you are here for a soul purpose.

We are all like onions with layers and layers of conditioning from our past experiences—pain, hurt, misery, hate, jealousy, envy, lust, resentment and unforgiveness. We are going to start by peeling layer by layer off the onion, so you can discover who you really are: an infinite being with no limitations and no longer being held back by old belief systems. I believe every human should reach their full potential with a heart full of fire to attract their hearts' desire.

In the centre of our being, underneath all the fabrications, there is a powerful force of unconditional love, light and truth that can heal us from our wounds, renew our minds, replace our hearts of stone with hearts of flesh and place a spiritual force in the centre of it empowering us to live in pure love with our fellow brothers and sisters despite race, religion, colour or creed. It's hard to even explain with words how much the force can transform us.

Before you start this amazing journey, I would like you to know, I care about you! Even though I don't know you, I do know you, because you are me and I'm you and we are one. I have your best interests at heart and want to see you flourish and blossom in all aspects of your life, to where you become a life vessel and you can overflow into others, shining the beauty of life onto those that may need some rays!

I urge you to follow the guidance in this book as we go through the tasks and activities steps by step. It's important to put the knowledge into action to enable you to discover the force within and build a relationship with it. It's vital that you follow the guidance to become fully awakened and driven by the force. Sometimes in life, we have to sacrifice people, things and behaviours to enable us to grow in life - out with the old, in with the new.

It's like a bucket full of crabs, one crab tries to climb out of the bucket and the others claw it back down. Many don't want you to grow, change or move on. They want you to stay the same and do the same old things. Sometimes it takes you saying goodbye to the old and leaving people behind for you to learn, grow and develop. I can assure you that by doing so, this eternal guide within will transform your life and release you from the negative strongholds that have conditioned you all of your life and lead you on a lighter path full of unfathomable miracles.

So just know that this journey may seem hard at times, but it will all be worth it in the long run. You'll be living a life in true freedom, peace, happiness, wealth and health, feeling a part of all living things and creating anything you put your mind to with no limitations. No more listening to the voice in your head telling you lies and limiting you. The time is now. This is where your life is about to change for the best.

Throughout the book, there will be affirmations to feed your subconscious because the more we feed the subconscious with positive affirmations, the more it will come to pass into our reality. Read the affirmations repeatedly and even try to remember them throughout your day whether you're brushing your teeth or driving. It can help you believe to achieve.

I am going to walk you through this journey sincerely, heart to heart, force to force from the power within. The power is available in the centre of your heart that is in all and through all, the beginning and the end, the alpha and omega. I will be illuminating everything that comes against you that keeps you enslaved by your lower self.

Life is a journey not a destination and through this journey you will become spiritually mature. You will experience life like you never have before. I need you to implement everything you learn to get the most out of this amazing journey. You are building a relationship with the force as you get to know me as I share in this book my deepest truths and rituals that I live by today, day by day, that have helped me to become the being I am today.

To prepare for this journey, here's your first affirmation:

I AM love.

I AM powerful.

Life has just started for me.

I AM able to do all things
in the power that lives within me.

I AM a new creation transformed
and transforming each day,
to become love.

Led by the spirit
rather than the flesh.

CHAPTER ONE: MY STORY

I am going to take you back to before my whole life changed for the better. I grew up on a council estate with a single-parent mum, witnessing drugs, crime and domestic violence. Not receiving any love at home, I soon found a belonging out on the streets with the older boys. Getting involved with drugs and crime at an early age, I became a menace to society and was placed into the care of the local authority. I was in and out of crack houses from the age of thirteen. Spending half of my life in prison, it became normal to eat with a plastic knife and fork. From gunshot wounds and being stabbed, to a machete attack that left me paralysed on my left side; I was left to die and nearly lost my life several times.

Living by the programme of my childhood experiences, the environment and the world…absorbing information and learnt behaviours from my parents and associates…I became a product of that environment. Later I became a mere reflection of the environment in which I was raised, lost and blind with no identity, trying to find belonging, acceptance and love—a hurt child, numbing his childhood trauma with drugs and alcohol.

So, it was at no surprise that I ended up in and out of prison for almost eighteen years. There reached a time when no one would come near me as I was a liability to myself and everyone around me. I had burnt all my bridges. My partner at the time, now my wife, was so afraid of me that she moved away to try distance herself from me. Then one night, in a hotel room, whilst on a heavy drinking binge and taking a cocktail of drugs with prostitutes, I tried to commit suicide by overdose. I woke up in the morning on my own in pure pain, lonely, lost and crying—the dark night of the soul. This experience was so painful I purposely left the hotel room that morning with the sole intention of creating havoc just so I can get arrested. Prison was a safe haven when things got too much for me on the outside. I was subconsciously being institutionalised, not being able to handle a lifestyle of responsibility in society.

I was back in prison, but this time it was different. I had come to that point in my life where I was finished with that lifestyle and the pain and suffering I had caused for myself and others. I had suffered physically and emotionally so much; either I would be killed or I would kill someone else and spend life in prison. There I was in a prison cell, broken and stripped down to the soul with no one and nothing, just my true unconditioned self. That's when I cried out to God from the centre of my heart. I had done this many times previously, but never with my whole self. This time was different. I gave my whole entire being. I went to sleep that night and in my sleep I was vibrating from head to toe in pure light. Pure ecstasy was running through my body. Something supernatural happened to me that night. It was as if I had died. My old self, the ego and the conditioned Dwayne had died and I was reborn, spiritually as a new creation. The truth.

Everything started to change from that moment. I was watching TV in the prison cell and it came to me: "What are these negative things I'm watching?" News that fuels anger, the overly sexualised music videos glamorising drugs and objectifying women, the obscenities, the scandals. I stopped watching TV. I changed the way I walked and talked. I disassociated from my old associates. The spirit inside me was more powerful than me and enabled me to create a new personality and reality. This transformation was a miracle from above. My whole life was changing, my whole perspective of life and the way I saw situations and circumstances. I stopped reacting to situations and instead I responded. I became in charge of my life. No longer was I a victim of my past but rather, I took full responsibility for my life and my actions. Before,

I had played the victim of my past and by doing so I had given my power away.

As I was transforming, I received insights to life and was guided by the force. It guided me towards changing my diet from normal foods to super foods. This enabled me to experience life in a whole new way with my body because being fully conscious was my priority rather than quick unhealthy fixes that would pull me into unconscious living and make me feel like crap. Bad nutrition can be an addiction just like alcohol, drugs, gambling and many other substances. I became a vegan for a while, then stayed a vegetarian. We can sometimes give little thought to what goes into our body and forget the simple fact that healthy, nutritious food is essential to survival. A car that needs petrol to move will breakdown if you pumped it with diesel. The body is not so different to a car in this sense. If you keep fuelling it with unhealthy food it may not break down instantly like a car would, but it certainly won't be at its peak performance. Feeding your body this way keeps you in an unconscious state eventually leading to a break down. Can you imagine a person making all these changes, from a reckless lifestyle of taking drugs and bad habits to becoming a health fanatic?

I was also being guided towards an immersion of meditation practices which became my everyday ritual. Fifteen minutes a day, in a quiet place, listening to my breath whilst mindful of how the spirit of light flows through me. It enabled me to become one with my true unconditional self and life. Being quiet and humble rather than being loud and proud, I started to build a relationship with "the spirit of light" inside me. It would whisper to me. That still, small voice of reason would lead me, direct me, guide me and protect me – it always had done but I just never noticed it because noticing requires one to be still and quiet to hear the voice of the heart.

I've been awakened to share this information and wisdom with you. It's divine order. It's not the man; it's the mission. You need to know that you are being fed poison, being told lies to keep you in slavery and prevent you from knowing yourself and the force within. As you will get to discover in Chapter 5, it is essential that we reprogramme ourselves and break free from the shackles that suppress us from the divine force - the same divine force that conspires to mature us and build a deeper and more congruent relationship with it.

I am not my body, my body is just my vehicle.

I AM a powerful infinite soul
being led by the spirit and the force.

I AM a servant of light and truth,
to make the world a better place.

I AM rooted in who I AM.

I AM rooted in unconditional love for all,
even those that have hurt me.

CHAPTER TWO: INVITATION TO CHANGE

D o you find yourself asking the question, "What is it all about?"

Doing the same old thing day in, day out, week after week: wake up, go to work, drive down the same road, drive past the same cars, see the same faces on the tube/metro, stop at the same coffee shop at the same time, even putting the same foods into your body? Thinking the same thoughts creates the same feelings that create the same emotions that create the same behaviours that create the same reality.

Do you have a void that you are trying to fill with money, materialism, relationships, drugs, alcohol, gambling or whatever vice you have chosen to bury your head in the sand with? Have you had enough of the same old you? Do you want to create a new reality, have a happy abundant life with joy flowing from the centre of your heart? Have you always had a feeling inside that there has to be more to life than this, that you are worth more than your current circumstances? It may be your job, your relationships, or your finances. You could even be bitter and angry with yourself for letting yourself go. Do you feel that you are living your life's purpose? Do you feel there has to be more to life than this? Do you wake up and just want to go back to sleep because life feels so bleak?

That is your spirit and soul crying out for change.

I can't answer these questions for you, only you can, and only you can make the decisions with action to make changes. You can contemplate your whole life or make the decision to change like I did, with leaps and bounds of action, fuelled by belief and wanting this more than anything in life because it IS your life. You are worth it; you just need to know your worth. All you need to do is build a deep relationship with your heart and listen to the still, small voice and let the truth set you free!

Where I am in this moment,
I AM whole and complete,
loved and loveable.

I AM light, love and truth,
through the force that has lit up inside me.

I AM limitlessly powerful
and I can move mountains
through the force
inside of me.

You need to make a decision that you want to change your life and the quality of it. With anything in life, if you want something, you need faith and to put dedicated work into it. If you want a good body, for example, to be healthy and feel good, it takes discipline: going to the gym, dieting, resting and for all of this to become part of your daily ritual.

It has taken discipline for me to write this book. Waking up at five in the morning every day to have the time to write. So now, people can be inspired and have the formula that will change lives all around the globe. It is amazing what we can do under the power of the force working inside of us; we can do all things in the force.

What I'm getting at is the first step of this journey: taking an hour or forty minutes a day for you, yourself and your relationship with the force to become more attuned to its likeness and to be able to harness its faculties. All the years you have been on auto-pilot doing everything your way, where has it gotten you? Burnt out, frustrated, battered and weary. We invest in all these exter-nal things in life— accumulating material objects, gaining status and wealth—but then, in the process, we sacrifice our precious self-time and energy, displacing it with the superficial. You owe it to yourself to set a time of day for you to be consciously present in the moment to build your relationship with the creator, gain-ing revelations, knowledge and sacred wisdom. Investing in the internal self means investing in the eternal self.

Studying the self is the best investment that a human being can ever make. Knowing oneself is knowing the force. I had to go through many trials to discover my authentic self, the force within. I was battered by life, up until I surrendered and tapped out from the ego, the story, the programme I had been living that was destroying me. I was my own worst enemy, living a life of pain and drama and self-sabotage. This went on for the better part of my life, being dominated by my lower self...the ego. I almost took my life a few times because I didn't like the person I had become.

Now the force within is working in my life, creating all that my heart desires in abundance, co-creating, instead of chasing and striving for external things to fill the void. Now, first and foremost I seek the kingdom of heaven and all else is added. When we first seek the things of this world, that's when things go wrong and we end up suffering. The force disciplines us when we go chasing people and things external to us. It's for us to strive and seek to know ourselves, that's when we get to know the force.

Realising that I was my own worst enemy, until I started loving my enemy; it was as if I was self- harming, causing hurt and pain, repeating the same things over and over again expecting different results. We are in a battle day and night with the fleshly nature, the carnal. It's hard to love ourselves when growing up. We may have been abused, hurt or treated badly, so we don't think much of ourselves because of this. We can repeat the same words to ourselves that others have spoken to harm us. I'm here to tell you the truth, so you can discover the force that will set you free.

In *The Matrix*, Morpheus says to Neo, "You take the blue pill, the story ends. You wake up in your bed and go back to living a lie of the programme of the world. You take the red pill, you stay in Wonderland, and I show you how deep the rabbit hole goes." The term "red pill" refers to a human that is aware of the true nature of the Matrix.

My friend, I am your Morpheus and you have a choice to take the blue pill, stop reading this book and go back to the programme that has been instilled in you, controlling and imprisoning you.

Or you can take the red pill, carry on reading this book and I will be your truth, light and life to lead you out of captivity through your mind, body and soul. Remember what I said at the beginning of this journey: it could be scary, exploring places that you haven't been before or doing things that the force is guiding you to do but the flesh is resisting. I'm talking internally and externally, discovering things about yourself or things about life. It can be very scary, especially when you find out something you have believed to be true almost your whole life is a lie. That can be very scary for anyone. This is why we are going to drive really slow on this journey so we can be conscious and remember the journey and absorb every experience.

It's like giving a baby solid food when it's not mature yet. It needs to grow before it goes onto solid food as it can't digest it and will likely throw it back as the food is too rich for the digestive system. We need to take time and grow.

It's all about timing and the different seasons. There is a time for eating, there is a time for digesting, resting and growing, but just remember, time and time again you will have growing pains. These are signs of development. Just like when one goes to the gym for the very first time, the next day you have sore muscles and aches. This is a sign that the muscles have torn and they are repairing and once they repair, they will get bigger and stronger.

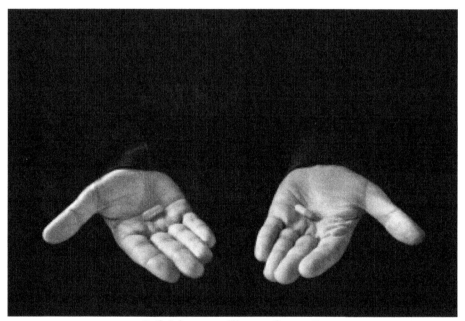

Which one will you choose?

I AM part of the whole of creation.

I AM life,
the seas the stars the moon and the sun.

I AM the I AM that I say I AM.

I AM all that there is and is yet to come.

I AM you and you are me
and we are all one.

I AM one with my true self
and every other living organism.

CHAPTER THREE: HURT AND HEALING

We have all been hurt in one way or another at some stage of our lives. If we got ill or hurt ourselves, we would go to the doctor and the doctor would diagnose the illness and then treat it. But the illness we're working with here does not have a quick fix; it's a slow, potent process of discovering the force. Part of this journey could become emotional as we detoxify our emotional pasts, hurts and painful experiences. Identifying them enables you to treat them by taking action to set you free—revealing it to heal it. Some people have a psychological story that has become a broken record for a number of years going around in their heads, when they think of the people that have hurt them. It prevents them from sleeping and eating and it destroys their lives by holding on to the pain.

Through our journey from childhood to adulthood we can get hurt physically, emotionally and spiritually from neglect, abandonment, abuse, rape, divorce, betrayal by someone you love...we all have been hurt in one way or another. I was neglected as a child and violently abused in a single-parent family, desperately wanting my mum's love and acceptance. When my mum split up with my dad, she started drinking heavily and taking her anger out on me. I was hurt and I carried resentment for my mother for the better part of my life, not realising this was a contributing factor to my behaviour and the quality of my life. My internal past pain was holding me back, preventing me from growing and being free.

The experiences of my childhood created stories and belief systems within my life. The victim story and other negative emotions kept me in bondage for many years, setting me on a self-destructive path and leading me to self-sabotage and hurting others around me at every opportunity. Some of us go through adversities in our lives and can carry that emotional energy with us for many years and the trauma destroys the quality of our lives. Some never become free and take it to the grave. Letting go will enable you to release and start the healing process. Whilst you are reading this you're probably holding on to some emotional energy from your past that has contaminated your psyche to the extent that it carries that emotional wound into the present moment.

You're repeating the story in your internal dialogue. You may not even talk about it and may not even know consciously that your personality is the way it is because you got hurt when you were a child or when you were in that relationship. Do you know what happens every time you think, talk and imagine your past painful experiences? Your body experiences it as if it's happening again. Consequently, you repeat this painful experience over and over again. So, you can imagine what is happening with your body: it starts to age, creates illnesses and diseases because it's repeatedly going through that same trauma time and time again.

We are built to be at ease with ourselves and others and if for any reason there is discomfort and dis-ease, then this will change the condition of the heart. The heart is a living organism. The relationship we have with it determines the relationships and the quality of the relationships we have with others and life. To live an abundant life, first your internal condition needs to be whole and complete with no resistance to the past events, just pure acceptance and unconditional positive regard and empathy for everyone despite any hurt or pain. It's going beyond the five senses and tapping into the spirit, the force that's in all and through all. Know who you are in the force and realise the vehicle that you live in—the body—is not you. That's why we become weak sometimes and can behave in certain ways. We become so identified with the body. But we are spiritual beings having human experiences. We can hurt each other unintentionally and intentionally and hold on to the hurt. What it does to the self is soul-destroying, eating away at one's psyche, even the biology, the physiology of the body, the atmosphere of one's internal and external environment is affected.

*I AM Love and I AM thankful
that the force forgives me
for all my wrong doings.*

*The past has no hold on me
and I AM free from condemnation.*

I forgive myself and those that have hurt me.

*I love them with
unconditional love.*

*I AM love
and love is my true essence.*

Many of us play the blame game in life for our current circumstances or situations, or what may or may not have happened to us in life. I played a victim story: I grew up on a council estate with my mum and witnessed her going to prison. I thought my life was destined to be that of a criminal. This was my programme, my story that kept me in bondage for most of my life. I played this character, being the victim of my circumstances, blaming everything and everyone for what was happening to me. Everyone but me of course.

It's only when the veils over my eyes lifted up that I received realisations and revelations that I was responsible for my life. I realised that I had the power to change things and do things differently. That's when my life changed. I became a victor rather than a victim, using my life mess as a message. We have all played these roles in one way or another—the show of life, the West End performances. We deserve Oscars!

When we blame others for our circumstances and situations, we are giving our power away and giving the power over us and our lives to the person or event. Saying "I'm in this state or place because of him or her or this or that" allows it to dominate the direction of our lives. The minute we accept and take responsibility, that's when we become empowered to take action and the past no longer has a hold on us and we, in turn, have learnt a new lesson.

Just imagine all the different stories that are running through our minds, all the different characters we play. There is a story being told right now about that person you have been blaming for hurting you, but stop right there. You, the force and I, together will shine the light of consciousness on that voice. By the end of this book, the force will have reconditioned your mind, so that the old record that has been playing in your mind for all these years will be replaced with the voice of truth, light and love. There will be a new voice taking over, the still small voice telling you new stories about yourself and others. The voice will be telling you the truth and things that make you feel good. If you hear things that don't make you feel good, you know the old self is trying to come back in. Just be conscious and speak good things to yourself and it will soon pass.

Here is the voice's message:

You are never alone even when you are going through some turbulence. Just know that it will pass. Come to that place of stillness and quietness, come and listen to me. Hold your hands near to your heart and listen to me speak to you. I'm as close to you as you breathe. Be still underneath the activity of the mind and just open me at a random page. You will find guidance; the words, the vibrations of them will change your state. Never feel alone; I am wherever you are. Wherever you go, I'm in the centre of your heart. Just remember to build a relationship with me, to spend some time with me. You need these times for the new consciousness to emerge. You will be free from the chatter and the thoughts. This is where we become one. I in you and you in me.

I AM whole and complete,
perfect and vibrant with love, joy and peace!

I will put out goodness, love and appreciation.

Today I will call three people
and tell them how much I love them,
how much they mean to me
and why!

We are very complex and emotional beings due to the fact that we live in this Earth-suit with our five senses and at times we can become so identified with it and its thoughts, feelings and emotions that they dominate and control our lives. Even all the external things can affect our five senses and the things we see, hear, smell, taste and touch can enslave us.

For example: A breakup or divorce can be a challenging time, especially when there are children involved. Unforgiveness and holding on to negative emotion towards an ex-partner, husband or wife, isn't good. This is toxic for the development of any child that may be involved, causing confusion as the child may love both parents and can feel the resentment and anger one holds for the other. Can you see how carrying any negative energy does not only affect you but everyone around you? You can't live life to the full whilst holding on to such a big weight.

I am going to leave you with a task before you begin the next chapter: go and forgive the person that has hurt you. Meet with that person if you can, look into their eyes and tell them how they hurt you and how much it affected you and your life. Then tell them that you forgive them and release all negative emotions towards them. If someone has hurt you and they are no longer alive, then write a letter and burn it, releasing all negative thoughts and emotions. Or if you are unable to meet with the person for whatever reason—it's too painful or it's not safe—then just write a letter and send it. If there's no way of reaching the person, then burn it. Sometimes it may even be yourself that you need to forgive for the wrong you may have done and the guilt you are carrying. Write a letter to yourself and tell yourself that you forgive yourself and you let go of any guilt, resentment, anger and shame. This is a therapeutic way of healing the wound that may be destroying your life. By doing this, you are letting go. So many times, there have been amazing outcomes on both sides and this forgiveness has changed the quality of life for both parties. There may even be a friend that you stopped speaking to for a reason you probably now have forgotten. Now all you need to do is pick up the phone and make amends and experience the power of forgiveness.

Have you ever been shopping before and carrying heavy bags and you can't wait to get to your destination because they are so heavy? When you get there and put them down, you feel so good, you feel so light. This is the same effect. You walk around your whole life carrying this burdensome bag of unforgiveness but the minute you put it down, you become light and free.

"Forgive them for they do not know what they do."

How are you? I hope you are still with me, still conscious and present and digesting this wisdom. What can get in the way and disrupt you from transforming? Fear. Fear is the absence of love and love casts out all fear. Fear is the essence of death. In later chapters I will go into the biology and physiology of what happens when fear and other negative emotions enter the body—not just the body, but the whole energy field. Why do we fear? Fear of rejection, fear of loss, fear of being late or even not reaching a goal, fear of death, fear of being abandoned, fear of violence. I'm saying fear but I'm going to put worry with fear, as they partner together. Once you let one in, then they are both in and they take over your mind. Why do you think they put so much fear content on the news? If they can get us in the fear vibration, then we are disconnected from the love frequency the result of which creates worry, stress, anger, anxiety and a lot of more negative human emotions.

Then we attract what we fear, because like attracts like. The goal is, minute to minute, hour to hour, day to day, to stay on the frequency of love, despite what is going on around us externally. Our internal states are what create our external environments. Yes, there will be adversities, trials and tribulations, but they have to come for you to grow; they are your greatest lessons and not your enemies. Obstacles are opportunities for you to grow, so next time someone does something to you or a situation occurs, ask yourself, "What can I learn from this situation? How can I grow from this lesson?" You might go through the same lessons many times until you grow. The minute we take off our glasses of past emotions that control our reactions, our present perception will be different, enabling us to create different realities.

Let's talk about the antidote to fear. I *love* you. Do you hear this word enough? When you do hear it, do you feel a real deep resonance behind it, the actual energy vibration from where it came from? Do you feel love or is it just empty words? We use this word in life like "hello", with no real authenticity or energy of love. Life has become so fast and robotic, we are not even in the present moment to feel the love in our own hearts, let alone send love out. We first need love within. We have become a soulless generation of hardened hearts, self-centred and lacking real love.

The question is, do you love yourself? Can you look in the mirror into your eyes, the windows of your soul, and honestly say, "I love you" and mean it? If you can, that's great! If you can't, or you can but don't feel the love, I urge you to repeat it every time you look in a mirror for the rest of your life. You will find that with time, the tight knots around your heart begin to loosen one by one and when they do your reflection will utter these words with total conviction.

Love of the self is the most important ingredient in life. I'm not talking an ego-driven, vain love of what you see, but a love for your whole being, mind, body, spirit and soul. Imagine trying to make lemonade without lemons, you simply can't, the same way you can't live life without love for yourself and others. You can't live a life of abundance, joy, happiness, peace and forgiveness without the foundation of life. Once you have love for yourself, you can put love out, but how can you put love out if there is none inside for you to share? You can't, because then you start manipulating love and attention from others: "If you behave like this, I will love you," or "If you do that, I will love you," or "If you don't do that, I won't love you." Those are conditions of worth.

The only way you can experience the love I'm talking about is by connecting to the force as the force is love and love is the force. Then you can share that love with others. It's a love that can't be expressed with words; it's a spiritual invasion of the heart, an inside job of the force, the truth, the light and the life. If you don't go within, you go without.

Love is the most powerful force in the universe. The energy of true unconditional love can bring miraculous signs and wonders to one's experience of life. Love is a vibrational frequency that is so powerful that it gives life because it IS life. Without love, we are death and dying. Once harnessed and expressed, it becomes a vehicle to heaven, but it stays rooted despite all the annoyances and distractions around us.

Staying rooted is very important, as the more rooted you are in love the more you will receive your heart's desire and when the storms come, you will still be standing like a big oak tree. Stay rooted and have compassion.

We live in a world today full of conditions and we become conditioned by others through manipulation or other forms of falsehood. This stems from fear. When you are living by the force, you are able to love others and everyone around you. Love is a vibration that comes out of the centre of your heart.

Where I am is loving and forgiving!

The past is gone and all we have is the now.

I forgive all who have hurt me in the past.

I hold only positive thoughts, feelings and emotions towards the whole of humanity.

I will go and forgive anyone that I have been holding negative emotions towards.

My mind and heart only filter love and forgiveness.

All is lovely and perfect in my world.

ACTIVITY
Family Tree

It is important to take a step back from the noise and just evaluate different aspects of life. In this activity we are going to evaluate our relationships. Below is a relationship tree. Fill out the names of your family members in the tree and score your relationship with that person using the key. Once you're finished look at how you can enhance your relationship with some of those low scoring family members. It is OK not to feel like you need to improve your relationship with everyone. You can just focus on the relationships that matter the most to you.

But equally, as we discovered in chapter three, if a relationship is creating a burden of resentment, anger or pain within you, this might be a good time to let go off that heavy load so you can truly break free from the shackles of those emotions. Just be honest with yourself.

Tip*: As you go through the scores ask yourself "Why have I given this person this score?" "What happened?"* From there you can think about what you will do to improve the relationship and how you will do it.

NOTES

CHAPTER FOUR: CARING FOR YOUR SOUL'S VEHICLE

Have you got a car? Do you remember how when you first got your new car, you would wash it, take good care of it, check it over and over again for any scratches or dirt. It was your baby and you looked after it. You took care of it.

Part of loving yourself is looking after your vehicle, the body that needs to carry your soul and spirit around. We need to be conscious of the food we eat and the drinks we consume that have pesticides, additives and other agents. These drugs are highly addictive, keep us addicted and keep us enslaved. There are so many products that we put on our skin or hair. Many creams, shower gels, makeup and toothpastes are also damaging to our bodies. All these substances are entering our bodies in one way or another and can be toxic to our minds, bodies and souls. Whatever enters the body affects the human consciousness.

Throughout my journey I have been guided by the force to cut out certain foods. I have experimented and researched. I used to be 14 stone and now I'm 12 stone. I lost all that excess weight. Now I feel alive, light and conscious of life.

Considering I was addicted to cigarettes, alcohol, crack cocaine and heroin, it's a miracle that I am living on such a higher level of consciousness and am now extremely conscious of what enters my body. This is because I want to be awake, effective and vibrant to serve humanity. I can't do that if I'm not on a higher frequency. To enable me to be on a higher level of consciousness, I need to put super foods into the living temple—the body.

Just remember that our bodies are vehicles for our spirits and souls, so it's not good for us to become so attached to the body and identify with it as though it was the entirety of who you are because who you are is so much more than your body. You are a spirit and soul having a human experience, an expression of life in physical form, but you want to keep that physical form in good shape, you want to make a good vehicle for your soul.

Food is the hardest addiction to tame as we need to eat to survive, but the question is how much and what do we eat? In society today, you only have to look around to see obesity is on the rise. Sugar and coffee are two main socially accepted addictions in the world and they are destroying lives. There is so much sugar in alcohol and it's just that which keeps us unconscious. Caffeine stimulates your heartbeat and brain. Due to this stimulation, when we want to slow down and meditate, it's more difficult to switch off, disconnect from the body and connect to the force.

I cut out bread, pastry, pasta, rice, chocolate, sugar, cheese and all other dairy products. I also stopped eating packaged processed foods and deep fried, oily food. No sugar-based fizzy drinks, coffee or alcohol. I started fuelling my body with the right liquid. I started consuming healthy organic food and drinking alkaline water. This change enabled me to travel light and be the light because of the vibrational frequency of consuming healthy food.

You're probably wondering what frequency has to do with food? Consider the importance of the Sun as a source of energy for all living things on Earth. Without the Sun, plants, animals and mankind will seize to exist. The Sun transmits a high vibrational energy into these living things and we in turn benefit from this vibrational frequency when we pick from a tree or pull from the ground fresh, organic fruits and vegetables. We are quite literally nourishing our body (both physical and spiritual) with food that is high and rich in nutrients from the Sun.

When we eat junk food, we tend to fall unconscious, feel heavy and operate from the lower frequency—the human nature. This food is often processed to the extent that little nutritional and vibrational energy is present for us to actually benefit from hence we feel sluggish and unable to move after devouring a burger or pizza. This prevents us from operating from the higher self. When eating and drinking higher frequency foods, you travel light and attract the light because like attracts like.

Unconscious eating. Unconscious mind.

I am not my body but I will look after it,
treat it well and put healthy food and water into it.

I will speak good and positive things to it
and protect it from any hurt.

I AM light and love so I will look after my body
as the body is my vehicle,
so I can express my soul and spirit through it.

I am not my body,
my body is just my vehicle.

I AM a powerful infinite soul,
being led by the spirit, the force.

I AM a servant of light and truth,
to make the world a better place.

I AM rooted in who I AM,
I AM rooted in unconditional love for all,
even those that have hurt me.

Fasting is a great way to enhance your awareness and connect to the force as it cleanses your body and helps you focus. Fasting is not just good for your body but also for your spirit and soul as it clears all the channels and you become light and the focus is on the unseen rather than the seen. You gain clarity and its good to pray in this time as it enhances the connection and the relationship to your higher self. This is because you are no longer unbalancing your body with stimulants and depressants. Yes, I know the body is telling you "Forget that!" because the body wants to be in charge. This is why fasting is so important because it's disciplining the body and showing the body that the spirit is in charge. Set one day a week or a few days a month or whatever suits you, but just remember it helps you to connect to you and if you are connected to the force, then you can do all things.

Benefits of fasting:

- Promotes detoxification
- Improves insulin sensitivity
- Rests digestive system
- Boosts immunity
- Clears mind & body
- Builds a deeper connection with the force
- Corrects high blood pressure
- May help to overcome addictions
- Promotes weight loss
- Resolves inflammatory response
- Promotes healthy diet
- Clears the skin
- Whitens the eyes

You can also fast from things like TV. Please do try it. By the end of this book, aim to have done a whole day and whilst you are fasting, be conscious of the powerful unseen force that lives in you and in all things. The force is life, it enables us to function and breathe, it gives the plants and trees life. Be conscious when you inhale new life. Just look at the beauty around you, nature and other people. Just take a bit of time to observe creation. You may have never done this before. Experience the bliss of fasting.

From this day, I will look after my body
as my body is my temple.

I will be conscious of what I eat and drink.

I will do regular exercise
and have equal rest.

I will love my body
and take care of it
and it will love me in return and take care of me,
as it's my dwelling - my home,
for the spirit of God to live in.

CHAPTER FIVE: REPROGRAMMING

W ho are you? Do you know yourself? Do you have a relationship with your true authentic self, the force within or have you just been running on autopilot? Have you been acting or behaving in a way to please others and at the same time sacrificing your true self in doing so? Has this been going on for so long now that you don't even know yourself because you may have played the role for far too long that you have become something you're not?

We go out into the world and start studying everyone and everything external to us to become just that—monkey see monkey do. Some students study to be a doctor, lawyer, bricklayer or plumber because it is in the family history and the pressure has been placed on them to be the same. So, they end up doing something with their lives that they don't want to do so they can please others. This is called an "external locus evaluation", sacrificing one's own beliefs, values or personality to please others.

The most important relationship is the relationship we have with the force. Knowing the force and studying ourselves. We as human beings are so quick to study things external to us, yet the most valuable and powerful subject to study and invest in is in ourselves, the force. Have you heard the saying "Know thyself"? Knowing yourself erases any fear and limitations, enabling you to harness the power within, create your own reality and know your immortality.

As for you, you are not your name given at birth. You are not your eighty percent water or your bones, your hair or your teeth. No, these are just elements of your human body.

When NASA went to the Moon, the astronauts had to wear spacesuits to survive in the atmosphere. The body you reside in is your Earth-suit; you are an infinite being, a spirit having a human experience. But we have forgotten this through birth and have been programmed to think otherwise, believing that we are our bodies and that we are limited to the body's five senses, believing lies about the world, about ourselves and what we are, who we are and what we can and cannot do. These are all limitations imposed upon us over time. Growing up, we can become conditioned by environment, people and family culture.

Knowing myself is knowing the power within.

Knowing I AM a spirit
that can move this physical world,
by knowing the truth of who I AM,
in the power of who I AM.

I AM the truth, the light and the life.

I AM powerful in the truth of who I AM.

There was an eagle that had been shot out of the air and it left behind an eaglet in an old derelict barn on a farm. There was a flock of ducks that lived nearby and the eaglet started to integrate with the ducks, soon becoming a full-grown eagle but behaving like a duck. Then one day this eagle looked up and spotted an eagle soaring through the sky. It wished and dreamed it could do the same. The eagle was so conditioned that it believed it was a duck and became restricted with the limitations of the ducks, never to fulfil its dreams and full potential due to the conditioning of its environment. *"You are the company you keep."*

This story is true for so many of us today. We have become products of our environments, putting limitations on ourselves through other people's belief systems and conditioning. You are a unique, special and talented soul with many gifts—not just natural but supernatural. It is your birth right. We are taught that we have our five senses and those are our limit. Let me tell you something, you are a powerful infinite being in the force and can do all things, with unlimited power and potential that can create all possibilities. What have you been telling yourself? The story you have been telling yourself is distorted due to the conditioning and environment, taking on other people's belief programmes. It's not what others think of you; it's what you think and believe about yourself that creates your reality.

We become conditioned from birth through the world's programmes, by institutions, the education system, media, religion, the banking system and industries such as Big Pharma. We are in one big programme. It's designed to imprison us and for us not to question it, but to just get on with it. What is it?

We are like sponges from birth, just absorbing information and data that's far from the truth. We are constantly bombarded with false information that prevents us from tapping into the unlimited source of intelligence. Through our journey in this book, we are squeezing the sponge dry of all the past conditioning belief systems and programming. Then we are soaking it in the river of life that is pure light, truth and love so that your soul will know and absorb the living water of life. You will then become conscious of your whole being, your thoughts, feelings and emotions, the energy that flows in and through your body, and you will start to respond rather than react to people, situations, circumstances and events. Once soaked in the river of consciousness, life will never be the same again.

It's our past experiences that have created our emotions and this is why we react to situations and circumstances the way we do. We have the glasses of our emotions from past experiences over our eyes. The past then is influencing the decisions and choices you make daily. For example, every relationship you have been in where your partner has cheated on you, you may make judgments and have issues surrounding trust in future relationships. Then fear, worry and insecurities come in the lower frequency, creating the same mistakes due to your past experiences.

Through this journey, you are going to let go of your past and your old self, and let the force renew your mind. As we go deeper into this journey, you will start experiencing things that I have talked about. These are just signs of growth and coming to a new consciousness where things start to become visible. You will start noticing things that have always been there but you just hadn't noticed because you've been on autopilot, living unconsciously on fast forward.

I'm so humbled that you are gradually shifting and changing your perspective on life. You're vibrating on a higher frequency now as you are living with increased consciousness and implementing the knowledge and wisdom into your life. As you grow and mature, you discover that life is a school, a university in the universe, and it always has been, yet we have been in a deep coma, on autopilot.

As you connect with me, you are like a radio receiving my energy, my thoughts through this book. Before our thoughts leave the physical body, they create a change in the biology of the body. If we are dwelling on negative thoughts, the thoughts create chemicals within the body that will germinate negative feelings which eventually create a negative emotion. This can then create illness, disease and even contribute to death. Life and death are quite literally in the thought.

The ego is the part of us that is trying to be something that is against our true nature. It is nothing but an accumulation of past experiences and stories that are on repeat, trying to play different characters to fit in and be accepted. It plays the victim, with an incessant need to be right and will lead a person on a self-destructive path under the illusion that everything he or she says or does is right regardless of whether it is or not. It will fight to get to the top, lie, steal, manipulate, murder, rape to fulfil its human desire. We have been destroying ourselves from all the lies we have been fed from the beginning.

If we have a negative experience and ponder the situation negatively over a long period of time then it turns into a mood and this manifests into our personality-reality. This is why it's so important to be in pure consciousness and illuminate any thoughts that are not in alignment with the spirit of the force. Think of love, truth, light, nobleness, peace, kindness and gentleness.

On the other side, thinking positive thoughts creates life through the mind, body, spirit and soul. Through the same way negative thoughts can create illnesses and diseases, positive thoughts can heal the body. This is scientifically proven. Our thoughts are alive and powerful, creating our future reality. Have you seen the Walt Disney cartoon where the paintbrush starts painting Mickey Mouse, then Mickey Mouse comes alive, then Donald Duck and then the whole picture comes alive? The paintbrush is our thoughts and our thoughts have the power to manifest anything into existence.

Our thoughts let out electromagnetic forces into the universe of all possibilities. Our hearts let out five thousand times more than the brain as the heart is the founder, the mental generator, the person. Whatever is going on with the heart, that's what is going to dominate the quality of the life of the individual. Have you heard of the saying, "As a man thinks in his heart so is he"? Our thoughts become things. They not only materialize, but we can also receive information and put information out, positive and negative. In this way, people are like computers linked to the internet. Our thoughts attract whatever they submit; they attract circumstances, events and people into our reality.

When I used to be enslaved by my lower self, my five senses, my life was dominated by my thoughts and they used to enslave me. This was because my belief system was from the programming of my past and that was the foundation of my life. What you need to understand is, your thoughts are virtually dominated by the heart, so the condition of the heart determines the nature of your thoughts and words. What's on the tip of a man's tongue is the overflow of a man's heart.

64

I AM powerful and can do all things
through the desire of my heart.

I AM an infinite, powerful being
with unlimited potential.

I AM love, light and truth,
whole and complete,
not lacking anything or striving for anything,
as I AM everything there is and is to be.

ACTIVITY

Life Map

One of the things that really helped me to evaluate my life whilst in prison was to write down certain milestones in life that affected me the most. From the first memories I had of being thrown from pillar to post in the social care system to certain events that led me to turn my back on a life of crime. Even now, as a successful entrepreneur, I revisit these memories on a life map to help me to appreciate the complexities of life, the relationships, the hardships but most importantly to help me recognise if something that has happened in the past is holding me back today. I continue to write down key events that have shaped my present day to remind myself that it's not always doom and gloom and that we can indeed retrace and heal from past wounds.

For this activity I want you to begin by focussing back on some of your earliest memories. Keep it to main events that sparked intense emotions. Intensely emotional memories have a tendency of being stamped as traumatic or in the case of good memories make you feel incredibly nostalgic. Whether the events are good or bad, briefly write them down because they all matter. You don't have to do this all in one sitting - in fact I urge you to take your time. Whilst you write each event, I want you to recognise how these events have shaped your present day and how they may be affecting the way you behave.

Tip: On your quest to map your life, *when you come across a time you that's still affecting you today or that you haven't quite let go off, ask yourself, why is this still affecting me today? What do I need to do to heal from this? How will I do these things?*

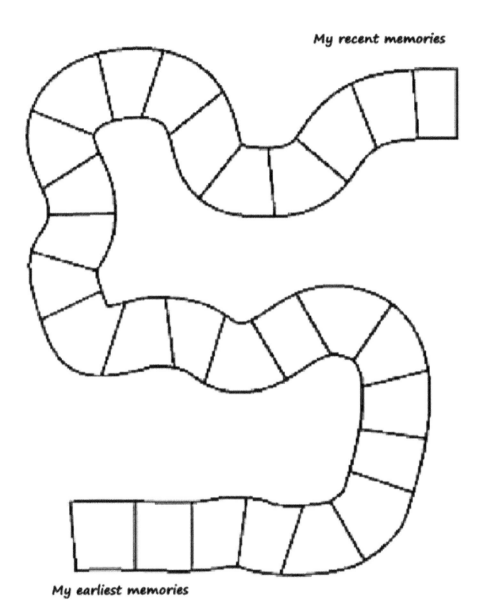

My recent memories

My earliest memories

NOTES

CHAPTER SIX: COMING TO CONSCIOUSNESS

The condition of your heart will determine your vibration, so guard your heart, as it is the wellspring of life. What happens when you go to the hospital with an injury? They check your pulse by putting a gadget on your finger to read the vibration of your heart to find out the beats per minute. Imagine your heart being taken out and it pulsing in a still swimming pool? It would produce ripples to the edges of the pool.

Now imagine that same pulse is happening every second of every minute of every day. You can't see it with the naked eye, but it's still pulsing.

What determines the condition of a man's heart is the vibration. If there is any unresolved hurt, pain, resentment, anger or any other emotions from the past that is still residing in one's heart, that impacts the quality of one's life. By picking up toxic emotions through life's trials and adversities changes the vibration of the heart. Unresolved issues create a poor condition for one's heart. One of the earlier chapters is on forgiveness because not forgiving will contaminate the heart, and if the heart is wounded this will create a poor quality of life. The revelation here is yes, your thoughts create your feelings and your feelings create your emotions. We have been created in the image of the creator, therefore, we are creators through the vibration that we put out from our hearts and minds. When the heart and mind work cohesively, the power of creation happens and it creates our reality without us realising it.

You are responsible for the vibration of your heart and its conditions. How do you do this? By healing any wounds, loving yourself and others, thinking loving positive thoughts. By living within the centre of your heart, you enable the force to help you live by the fruits of the spirit—love, joy, peace, forgiveness, patience, gentleness, goodness, kindness, fruitfulness and self-control. Without the force of truth, light and love, we tend to get lost and our hearts become hardened in this cold and dark world. We can only survive with the force as we are nothing without it, just flesh and bone. It's being conscious of this and having the knowingness that we are not on our own. In this cold world, it's not what's going on externally that matters, it's your internal reality that creates your external reality.

By meditating, we disconnect from the body. By disconnecting from the body, we go into the world of all possibilities. By becoming still in the presence of the power of now there is no dialogue after some practice. We become free from the voice that's constantly controlling our lives, telling us things in our heads from past experiences that have shaped our personality-reality.

By meditating, you start to build a relationship with your heart, the still, small voice within. This voice can only be heard when you are centred and present in the now; that voice is the force. The more time we spend in the meditative state, the more intertwined we become with the force. The more conscious we become, the more power we have to create our hearts' desire and not re-create the horrors of our pasts.

Meditation enables us to connect new neurons that wire together and fire together, creating new circuits in the brain. It helps your immune system, aids anti-aging and has many other fantastic health benefits, but the most valuable one is that it connects you to the force, the power of creation.

Meditation has been a ritual for me since my spiritual awakening. It has helped me discover who I really am and my capabilities, from natural to supernatural. I believe this should be taught in schools at a very young age and we should practice this with our children.

I started mediation in 2012 and I have made this part of my daily ritual ever since. I couldn't even begin to explain with words how much this has changed my life and the experiences I've had throughout this time. If you're thinking, "What's meditation and how do I start?" then just start by sitting on a chair or on the floor in a nice comfortable quiet place. Sit up so your spine is straight and if you are sat on a chair make sure the soles of your feet are flat on the ground. Become aware and centred and start to really feel and read your breathing by inhaling and exhaling. Listen to the background for the birds or the cars in the far distance then start to count down from a hundred. If your mind wanders off or begins to identify with the voice in your head you will lose count so then start again. After you get to zero, then you just stay centred and rooted and just become what can only be described as nothingness. If you continue practicing this, your life will change in a more meaningful way; you will become conscious of the force of creation. If you're new to this and need direction whilst meditating, you can always go onto YouTube and listen to a guided meditation as it will talk you through it.

Meditation can take us out of that unconscious, autopilot state and into consciousness. Consciousness is the state or quality of awareness or of being aware of the external surroundings whilst still being conscious of one's own thoughts, feelings and emotions. The ability to experience or to feel wakefulness, having a sense of self and being conscious of your internal dialogue.

There is a difference between doing things with unconsciousness and being present in the moment. There is a difference between being and doing. Doing things in an unconscious state means you have a deep identification of thought about the future or the past, becoming lost in an illusion within your own mind. Unconsciousness is like doing something on autopilot, sleepwalking, striving for an outcome of a situation, being driven by low frequency thoughts feelings and emotions. It's even the illusion, the obsession of seeking 'high' positions, thinking these things will make one feel whole only to later find out that they don't. Unconsciousness is not being still for the present moment, because we are worrying about the past or future or live in discontent with the present moment and the true essence of life.

Always make time to just be still.

The same force that ignites your heartbeat makes the seed that you put in the ground grow into a beautiful flower. Yes, it's amazing what we are, but yet we have fallen asleep in a coma. By the end of this book, you will be a fully realised, awakened conscious being, led by the force, the light, the truth and the life. You can start by simply being conscious when you're eating. Consciously make an effort to fully commit to the present moment, anticipating every bite, appreciating the richness and taste of every flavour instead of rushing to eat so you can get somewhere or do something. Similarly, when going for a walk just feeling the wind on your face, listening to the birds, connecting to the force and feeling that moment of bliss where there is no past or no future. Just now. Afterall, all we have is the power of now!

We are in a battle to stay conscious in this new age of technology, becoming a computer generation, distracted from being —that's right, BEING. We are constantly doing, striving to get, to have or to become, burning ourselves out with frustration. We are not content with ourselves, because we don't even know our true selves. If we did, we wouldn't be creating pain and suffering for ourselves and others. We are distracted with what we can see, taste and touch when we should be more concerned with the unseen. What we see is temporary and the unseen is eternal. If we just slow down and become still, we could connect to the power of the force within.

I AM pure force-consciousness,

the orchestra of all matter.

I AM Love. I AM peace. I AM one with all living life force!

I AM the force and can do all things

in the name of love, hope and faith.

I AM growing spiritually and I AM enlightened.

My light is getting brighter in force.

Consciousness is like the ocean and we are a bottle floating on the surface of the ocean. As the bottle bobs along it contains a little bit of the ocean within; the powerful force of life that enables us to be limitless and create our heart's desire. But we have become so identified with the bottle we have forgotten the ocean inside of us, the force. Are you consciously reading this book, gaining the information and processing the words, or are you in and out of consciousness, thinking of the past or the future? Perhaps you're thinking about what happened earlier in the day or last night? When you aren't in the present moment to experience life in a wakeful state, you are unable to receive insights and revelations due to being unconscious. By doing so, you miss the signs and signals from the force that's trying to guide us through life's journey.

Mind over matter rather than matter over mind. Why do you think we find ourselves drained and banging our heads against the wall? Because we are putting our trust into matter. Absolute madness. I did this for many years, putting all my trust in *doing* rather than *being* and tapping into the infinite power of all possibilities. The thing is, we are creative beings, whether that's in a negative or positive way, whether you are consciously aware of this or not. Whichever side of the duality we choose to ponder on, the creation is our reality.

Force-consciousness is life. Without it, there is no life. From when we are force-conscious, we are aware of what we are thinking. We are no longer identifying with our thoughts. We gain clarity that we are the consciousness rather than the thoughts. Force-consciousness enables us to be the watchers of our internal and external environments/circumstances without being identified. Being the observers of the story, we think of ourselves as the voice in our heads, the characters that have been made up and we play the roles of who we think we are. You have been running on a programme that's being dictated by other people's views, opinions and beliefs—the world's version of how you are supposed to be. Down to the way you walk, talk, dress and behave, your religion, work and studies, you have been conformed to the product of who you are and have become. You have been imprisoned by unconscious programming and don't even realise it.

When your thoughts and emotions work together, they create feelings. There is a field in the atmosphere that reads your feelings. That is the prayer language of the universe. This is why we need to be conscious of the feelings that we are creating. This is why the force teaches us about the power of love and to love with all your mind, body and soul – to love your neighbour as yourself. Why? It knows the laws of the universe and how love is the most powerful frequency in the universe. Love's high frequency is the living force of humanity. We should be on this frequency every minute of every day so we are in cohesion with the power of creation. When we are in this power, when we believe in it whole-heartedly, we can do all things.

I hope you are with me, still enjoying this journey. I hope one way or another life is becoming more "vibrant" for you. Do you understand how important it is to be conscious of our thoughts? They are the language to the brain and emotions are the language to the body? When these two become one, powerful experiences manifest from the unseen to the seen. Whether you are conscious of the vibration coming out of your heart or not, it's creating your environment and reality. We will reap what we sow. What we put out, we get back shaken and stirred. Everything is governed by a simple law of cause and effect.

Guard your heart as it's the wellspring of life! Protect yourself from being hurt! When one is inflicted with a wound close to the heart, it creates a frequency that affects the thoughts, feelings and emotions inside them that creates their reality.

The force resides in the centre of your heart. It's the infinite power of the whole universe, the beginning and the end, the Alpha and Omega. We need to be still for the present moment and know that it is the divine force.

A relationship with the force within will be the most important relationship you can ever have. When you know yourself and your own heart, this realisation of the force is the start of life's mystical adventure into a life of oneness.

This is the beginning of a powerful experience called life, where you have a connection to the now and with the oneness of all that there is and all that was and all that is to come. You become part of the great big orchestra of life, playing your part and being conscious of the tune of the vibration that you are playing from your heart. This vibration is the manifestation of creation. I hope you are with me and you understand that your heart is the direct creator of the vibration that is going out into the field of all possibilities.

You have come to receive this book through the law of attraction. This book is made up of energy and you were meant to come across this information, to take you to the next level of your life by changing your vibration as you are working through each chapter. We are energy. Everything in the whole universe is made up of energy. We are all vibrating at a different frequency. The frequency we vibrate at manifests the people, events and circumstances in our lives.

When using a radio, if you want to listen to jazz, you would need to tune into Jazz fm. You couldn't tune into Rock FM and listen to Jazz. Just pause for a moment and think how this analogy relates to us.

We are like radio stations constantly putting out a frequency that's going to attract and manifest our reality. Have you ever heard the saying, "You are the company you keep"? This is correct because when you come together with others, you become part of that one energy field. Have you ever been in a car full of people in the winter and seen what happens to the windows? They steam up! Have you ever touched someone and received an electric shock?

Like attracts like. We are sending out frequencies, vibrations, every minute, every second of our lives. This attracts the same people, circumstances and situations into our lives. We understand this as being the Law of Attraction but it is also the Law of Cause and Effect. Man reaps what he sows and we are sowing right now with the vibration that is pulsing from the heart and the brain, with the electromagnetic force that is going out into the field. We are sending out data and receiving data all the time. We need to be conscious of what we are pondering on, our dialogue and what is in our heart, as that same electromagnetic force that comes from within us goes out to the universal field of all possibilities.

Life becomes so magical when you start living from pure consciousness. From here, you will begin to experience the unbelievable, or as I like to call it, ´the sweet synchronicities of life´.

Anyone that knows me well will be familiar with my attraction to the number seven. Anything that has seven in it is a sign for me and always has been. One morning in prison, I woke up feeling in a really good place both spiritually and emotionally. Before I went to my education class in the prison that day, I wrote down my girlfriend's number, ripped the page out of the notepad and called her before going into class. Whilst talking to someone in class, a man approached me and said he had something for me. I was keen to finish my conversation but at the same time curious as I didn't know this man nor did I know what or why he wanted to give me something. He hung around in the library until I finished my conversation. Now when you're in prison and someone you don't know says they have something for you, you're mind goes to all sorts of strange places. Trying to anticipate what on earth this man had for me, I approached him and as I drew closer he said he had an interesting spiritual book for me. Phew! Before he had even proceeded to show me the book, I started to feel an over-whelming surge of excitement and began talking to him about synchronicity. He was looking at me as if I was crazy and the officers too were glaring at me in the same manner. Nevertheless, I continued to speak to this man, telling him about synchronicity and how this book was meant for me. he man handed over the book and as I held it in my hand I stood in absolute disbelief. What was on the front page? The number seven. I gave the man a hug who now had an assured look in his eyes that I had lost my mind.

I went back to my classroom thinking, 'If only they knew.' I sat down with the book, excited to read it. It was called *The Seven Spiritual Laws of Superheroes*. I thought to myself, 'Wait, I know this book.' When I looked, I saw that the author was Deepak Chopra. I was absolutely lost for words. I had written this book down on my wish list in my notepad and had asked my girlfriend to get this book for me two weeks prior and then this man I didn't even know came out of nowhere and handed me that very book! Later that same day, I reached into my pocket and pulled out the ripped piece of paper I had written my girlfriend's number down on that morning from my notepad back in my cell. On the back of the piece of paper, written across the middle was the name of the book.

This is the power of divine order, synchronicity. This is the power of the Force, bringing everything you need in life and it helps you to evolve into your true self. Sometimes that may be through a book or it may be through meeting someone to give you a piece of the puzzle of life.

On another occasion, I was in the car with my wife having a conversation about the ego and how we needed to dissolve it. It all started because half an hour before she was showing off our flat to visitors. As I'm speaking to her about the ego explaining how we are in war with it daily and how we need to be in the spirit rather than the ego, I shouted to her to stop the car. When she stopped, she said, "What?"

I said, "Reverse please." When she reversed, I said, "Look!" There, like an affirmation to our discussion, was a car with number plate that had the word "EGO" written on it.

Synchronicities are the communications from God, the universe giving you confirmation that you are on the right path and that you are conscious in the present moment in the power of now. It is a relationship and you have to be congruent in the power of now and in alignment with your soul's purpose. Then you will be in a meaningful relationship of correspondence with the oneness of life. Think of it as when you are speaking to someone and they respond; it's a two-way street. It's also a signpost that you are on the right track.

Life can become so mystical and creative when we become conscious and are awake to see life for what it really is. A world of all possibilities and adventures is revealed when we just slow down and become still and bring the heartbeat down and build a relationship with the heart. That is where that still, small voice waits to lead and support you. All we have to do is listen, but what we do instead is listen to the programmes that have been installed and running since childhood. These are much louder, with their limited beliefs, lies and falsehoods installed by the world.

People perish due to the lack of knowledge; they live a certain way because they do not know any different. Eat certain foods because that is all that is there and the body is addicted and accustomed to their use. Most people do not know otherwise; they watch TV programmes not knowing it is actually programming them, their souls, with subliminal messages and creates fears and anxieties. We are living in a cold world and if you don't become force-conscious and live wisely, then you will fall into a deeper coma and become your own worst enemy.

Where I AM is love.

All I see is love and empathy for humanity
as I know everyone is doing the best that they can
at their understanding and their evolution.

Even when others behave
in a manner that may not be appropriate,
I have unconditional love
and I will try to serve that soul in the best way I can.

They may have been hurt and that's why
they are behaving in that way.

This gives me an opportunity to serve a hurting
wounded heart.

THE TREE OF LIFE

Activity
Finding My Why

What

Most people have an idea of what they need to do to change their habits or achieve their goals. For example, when I kept ending up in prison, I knew deep down I needed to change my habits. The drugs, the alcohol, the crime, the abuse, it all had to stop.

How

Thinking 'how' you will do something needs a little thought. Taking my example, when I figured out what I needed to do to change, I became more open to understanding how I needed to do it. I began to read self-help books; I spent more time in the chaplaincy and solitary meditation and less time around negative influences. I kicked my addiction of drugs and alcohol by replacing each craving with a healthy alternative, until eventually I no longer had the urge to smoke or drink. But before I even got to this stage, there was one more powerful question I needed to ask myself...

Why

...Why? The answer to this question becomes the driving force, turning the cogs of the *'what?'* and the *'how?'*. Few people understand why they want to achieve their goals. It requires you to delve into the deepest level of thinking to understand your motivation for changing. It's beyond the materialistic, the desire for money and fancy cars. Finding your **'why'** is about attuning to the language of your heart. Your *why* could be to improve personal relationships for example, or in my case, it was so that I can make an impact in this world before I am gone and provide security for my children.

I want you to sit in a quiet place and ask yourself 'What is my why?' What is the thing that inspires me from within? What is it that motivates me to wake up and make me want to work hard for my goals? Think beyond material things like money and luxury, these don't come from your heart. Think deeper! What is the why that connects your soul's purpose to this world? From there you can then begin to plan what you need to do and how you will get there. There's no right or wrong way to do this. Maybe you want to start with what and how before you go to why? Either way, you should really commit some thought behind your reasons as this is what will excel you in achieving your goals.

NOTES

CHAPTER SEVEN: BECOMING LIMITLESS

Man will fight and kill in the name of God. Man will argue whose religion is right and whose is wrong. Man will twist and pervert and because of this, will destroy religion and humanity. We are our own worst enemies. The battle isn't with anyone external to us but with ourselves, the ego, the fleshly human nature. Our authentic selves, our divine force lives within. Whatever you want to call it, man will argue over that alone. I call it the force, some call it Jesus, others call it Allah, and some call it the divine, the universe; these are mostly man-made names that mean the same thing.

My religion is love, celebrating both the similarities and differences of this Earth-Suit we strut around. Everyone is my people as we are all one, made up of the same thing, all with the same struggles and deserving of inner freedom from the enemy within.

When we do build relationships with the force within our hearts, life becomes one big adventure, a world of all possibilities. Life begins when you have that relationship with the God within. We are nothing without the force, one spirit, one God.

The transformation is from the fleshly nature of the ego into the spirit of the force. The power is the spirit, the one source of all creation, the beginning and the end, the Alpha and Omega. This powerful light is the same intelligence that makes your heart pump 2,000 gallons of blood throughout your body each day and the same energy that enables a plant to grow, the same one that makes a wound heal and the same power that holds the planets in orbit. That spirit came in many men to show the way but those men got persecuted for being and living the truth and love.

Man is its own worst enemy, totally identified with the flesh, the human nature, focused on the seen rather than the unseen. We become so identified with the story of who we are as limited human beings that we forget that we can do all things in the force. Jesus said before his departure, "Very truly I tell you, whoever believes in me [the force] will do greater things than these." John 14:12 You will do greater than I, but this is when we are living in the spirit rather than the limited flesh matter.

A relationship with the force and the kingdom of heaven isn't out there in a man, woman or location but within the centre of our hearts. My influences have been from the Bible and the teachings of Christ and the crucifixion of myself to enable the force to take over and do the Father's will on Earth as it is in heaven. I'm not conformed to the things of this world, but instead keep steadfast in the renewing of my mind through the force that lives within. John 2:27 says: "As for you, the anointing you received from him remains in you, and you do not need anyone to teach you. But as his anointing teaches you about all things and as that anointing is real, not counterfeit—just as it has taught you, remain in him."

There is only one way to live life with happiness, joy, peace and abundance. This is plain and simple but our sinful nature, the ego, lower self or whatever you want to call it, makes it complex and wants us to suffer with daily drama. We just need to receive the force into our lives, let it speak through our hearts and take over our bodies as living sacrifices. Then we can receive its power and righteousness and positive loving energy to do its will on Earth as it is in heaven

The minute we want to hold on to the 'I,' we will suffer, as we will be operating from the old programmes that want to hold on to painful experiences and drama. The ego stays alive by telling stories in your own head and telling those stories to others. It has us behaving in a way to impress people. It will lie, gossip, and do whatever it can to be the best and put others down. The ego is our enemy. When we can connect to the force, we build a relationship with the whole of creation and stop identifying as 'me' or 'I' and we stop being separate from the collective of the whole. We become secure as we feel whole and complete because we are one with everyone and everything that we can see, taste and touch. The force has our best interests at heart because it is us and we are it and the body is just a vessel, a manifestation from matter.

It's when we malnourish our bodies by indulging in unhealthy habits, it's when we let the ego speak out louder and louder dictating our decisions every day and it's when we don't attend to that little small voice that emanates from the centre of the heart that we welcome the illusion and allow it to manifest. If we allow the manifestation to take its course then we start to believe the illusion and it becomes our reality, the programme. Being attuned to the programme rather than the force is why so often people take their own lives as they live in an unsatisfied, depressed and unconscious state; constantly tormented by the illusion rather than nourished by each breath taken in the present moment.

The same life force that transformed me is now leading me—the spirit of light, truth and power. The force has protected me and carried me throughout this epic journey since 19 November 1984 up into the present. I was released from prison on the 22nd August 2014 and took charge of my life, got married to my amazing wife and found a job. I started working on release for an agency as a labourer with full awareness that there were big things waiting for me ahead. I was content with my circumstances and creating great vibes. Whilst I was in that job, I met a man named Dave. Dave linked me with Neal and Neal, at the time, was doing a job for Jason Downs, a successful banker in little Marlow Manor House. I was employed by Jason from 2014 to 2016. This was my training ground for what was ahead. I had a senior position in a children's home whilst still on prison licence. Breaking all limitations, I delivered the **Hit the Road Jack Programme** which I had created within my prison cell. This is an A-Z on how to transform your life and become free from the old self, the enemy within. Now I have the keys to the prison that once kept me prisoner. I'm attending prisons all around the UK delivering motivational speaking and my bespoke *Hit the Road Jack programme*. Only five years after my release and I've now become the founder and CEO of www.RoadLight.co.uk and Community Interest Company www.7RoadLight.co.uk. Both organisations are a fundamental platform for self-discovery and are now awarded accreditation as an Open College Network centre.

Through these companies, our mission is to empower millions of lives by shifting the consciousness of humanity through books, online products, motivational speaking, programmes, courses, workshops and seminars, helping people discover the light within and enabling us all to live a life of abundance without limitations and with love, peace, joy, happiness, health and wealth.

I believe in the force that you can't see taste or touch but it's alive and it's here—the light, the truth and the life. Without being in a relationship with the force and being in coherence with it, life will never work and you have to work with life to be used as a vessel for the force.

This is when you realise that you have woken up to a living force that's always been there, but you have been sleeping in a coma of programming from the third dimension. Welcome to a glimpse of the fifth dimension and what's available to you. If you haven't shifted already throughout the journey of reading this book and implementing its lessons then do not fear. Shift itself has its time just as the seasons and the tide. Keep practicing, keep noticing, keep still and listen.

Now you understand, all that you have been looking for your entire life is inside. You no longer need to search and you can stop running around like a headless chicken and just be still – letting the force do all that matter stuff. You don't have to work hard, you just need to work smart as you co-create with the creator, the force, inside and outside of you. It will lead you, guide you, and shine its great light through you. Now go out there and shine your light.

HAVE A WONDERFUL ADVENTURE.

I AM living in the now.

I AM not the experiences of my past.

I AM creating my future from this moment.

*I AM my future before it manifests
into the physical realm.*

I AM all that I think I AM.

I AM what I feel and imagine I AM.

I AM responsible for my reality.

Printed in Great Britain
by Amazon